Maintaining Health And Wellness During Ramadan

Nourishing Your Body and Soul: Healthy Habits for Ramadan

Mohammed B. Saeed

Table of Contents

Introduction

Greetings and welcome to "Maintaining Health and Wellness during Ramadan," a thorough handbook created to assist people in maximizing their emotional, physical, and spiritual well-being during the fasting month of Ramadan. The Islamic lunar calendar's ninth month, Ramadan, is a time of great significance for Muslims all over the world. It is observed by fasting from sunrise to sunset as a means of spiritual cleansing and prayer.

Even while Ramadan is a time for introspection, bringing people together, and heightened devotion, it also offers special chances and challenges for those who are trying to stay well. During Ramadan, fasting means abstaining from food, liquids, and other physical pleasures from sunrise (suhoor) to dusk (iftar). This can have a big impact on a person's daily schedule, eating habits, and way of life.

To address the various facets of health and wellness throughout Ramadan, this book offers helpful advice, recommendations based on solid research, and comprehensive techniques to help people navigate the fasting season with resilience, vitality, and mindfulness. Using scientific research, professional insights, and Islamic teachings, this guide seeks to equip readers with the information and skills necessary to maximize their spiritual and healthful experiences both during and after Ramadan.

Starting with an introduction to the importance of Ramadan in Islam and the observation of fasting as a fundamental tenet of faith, we will examine several aspects of health and well-being in the context of the holy month of Ramadan in the ensuing chapters. We will explore the physiological impacts of fasting on the body, looking at both the possible health advantages and typical problems that fasters encounter.

During Ramadan, nutrition and hydration are essential for maintaining energy levels, supporting body processes, and fostering general health. Consequently, we will discuss doable tactics for keeping a healthy diet, maximizing water, and choosing wisely what to eat at suhoor and iftar, the pre-dawn, and post-sunset meals, respectively.

Exercise and physical activity are essential to a healthy lifestyle, but incorporating them into your Ramadan routine demands thought and preparation. We will cover how to fit exercise into Ramadan habits, modify exercise plans to accommodate fasting periods, and reconcile religious adherence with fitness objectives in this book.

Physical and mental health depend on sleep, rest, and relaxation, all of which can be negatively impacted by Ramadan due to altered daily routines and an increase in spiritual activity. We will discuss techniques to support sound sleep habits, control stress, and maintain mental well-being during the fast.

We will also talk about the medical consequences of fasting for those with pre-existing diseases and about particular groups like children, teenagers, pregnant women, and the elderly. Our goal is to encourage inclusivity, accessibility, and safety for all people who fast by offering advice on how to modify fasting practices to suit unique requirements and situations.

This book also highlights the value of community involvement, spiritual meditation, and social support networks in promoting health and wellness throughout Ramadan. We will discuss ways to develop inner peace, thankfulness, and mindfulness on an individual basis as well as how to promote a sense of solidarity, compassion, and belonging within communities.

In the end, "Maintaining Health and Wellness during Ramadan" acts as a guide for people who want to prioritize their health and well-being over their religious obligations. This book presents a comprehensive approach to fasting that honors the body, mind, and spirit, enhancing the Ramadan experience and encouraging lifetime vigor by fusing Islamic beliefs with scientifically proven health practices.

For everyone starting the journey of fasting during Ramadan, may this book serve as a source of motivation, empowerment, and direction, showing the way towards optimum health, wellness, and spiritual fulfillment.

Chapter One

Understanding Ramadan

Ramadan

One of the holiest months for Muslims is Ramadan, which falls during the ninth month of the Islamic calendar. The Holy Qur'an is said to have descended from heaven during this month "as a guidance for men and women, a declaration of direction, and a means of salvation."

Muslims follow a severe fast from sunrise to sundown during this month. During the day, they are not permitted to eat or drink anything, not even water. Fasting is a personal act of worship that deepens one's relationship with God. It is also a way to practice spiritual discipline and develop compassion for the less fortunate. After the day, iftar, a joyous supper, and prayer break the fast. After the iftar, it is traditional to visit family and friends.

Many Muslims visit the mosque and spend several hours praying throughout the month of Ramadan. Apart from the five daily prayers that form the foundation of Islam, Muslims also perform a unique prayer known as the Tarawih prayer, which is performed at night.

Muslims observe a unique night known as Layat al-Qadr, also known as the Night of Power, on the evening of the 27th day of Ramadan. It is thought that on this night, Muhammad received the Holy Qur'an for the first time.

Eid al-Fitr commemorates breaking the fast after Ramadan. Families and friends get together for joyous dinners and gift-giving. The impoverished also receive special presents.

How are the Ramadan prayers and fasts observed by Muslims?

When someone fasts, they often refrain from eating, drinking, and having sex from before the sun rises till it sets. For Muslims, all 29 or 30 days of Ramadan must be spent in fasting. In case you are incapable of fasting, you can donate or fast on non-Ramadan days. Eating breakfast is customary and regarded as a very honorable custom. Sundown fasting is typically broken with dates and milk, with a larger meal coming after evening prayers. Apart from the five daily prayers, another highly significant optional ritual is to assemble for extra communal prayers every month after the evening prayer. Tarawih is the name of this prayer.

What is Ramadan and when is it?

In the Islamic lunar calendar, the ninth month is the holy month of Ramadan. It is a month of social gatherings, devotion, fasting, and spiritual growth. One of Islam's Five Pillars is fasting during the month of Ramadan. Ramadan "moves back" by roughly 11 days every solar year due to the 12 lunar months being overlaid over the 12 solar months. The first day of fasting in 2024 is scheduled for March 11; however, because Muslim groups have different interpretations of this date, some may designate the month to start a day earlier or later. Similarly, the celebration of the breaking of the fast, known as Eid al-Fitr in the United States, might occur on different days based on cultural, familial, or personal preferences.

Around April 9 (dates may vary), the Eid celebration, which signifies the conclusion of fasting, is anticipated. It starts with a morning congregational prayer and ends with visiting relatives and friends. Many people would decide to take the day off as Eid is a holiday that lasts for the entire day, not just the morning prayers. According to the Academic Coursework and Religious Observance Policy, this makes it an excused absence. On Eid, some people could choose to go back to work or school and take tests. The two days after Eid are also observed as holidays in several cultures.

Important lessons learned:
• In 2024, Ramadan will fall between March 10 and April 9.
• In 2024, the window for fasting is 5:46 a.m. and 6:48 p.m. during the start of Ramadan and from 4:52 a.m. to 7:21 p.m. by Ramadan's conclusion.
• Some people might begin their fast earlier and end it later.

Variability in practice:
It is also usual for different interpretive schools to place different time limits on the beginning and end of the daily fast. For example, on a college campus, some Muslims may break their fast right after sundown, while others may wait for ten minutes or longer. It is often preferable not to inquire about someone's fasting practices because some people may feel more at ease discussing their reasons for not fasting, which can be quite private and personal.

Although milk and dates are traditionally fast-breaking foods, there is a great deal of ethnic variation in the cuisines that people choose to eat throughout Ramadan. Certain cultural customs reserve the huge, hearty pre-dawn meal for fast-breaking meals, and instead favor light fare. While some cultural traditions practice massive fast-breaking meals, others may observe merely a light pre-dawn meal. In certain modern societies, eateries, and cafes operate throughout the clock, giving rise to a gastronomic "nightlife."

Ramadan is observed differently depending on the culture, in addition to fasting and breaking of fasts. While some may view fasting as their main ritual, others may view it as an opportunity to socialize, visit loved ones, and engage in more acts of worship, such as prayer or reciting the complete Qur'an during the month.

Both great variety in the manner and degree of observance and unanimity exist.

• Everybody experiences Ramadan's challenges differently.

Certain individuals are exempt from fasting, either temporarily or permanently.

It can be awkward to inquire about someone's fasting habits for a variety of reasons.

• One may break their fast in case of an emergency.

What is the significance of Ramadan

One of the five "pillars of Islam" (the others being the profession of faith, daily prayer, almsgiving, and the pilgrimage to Mecca) is the month of Ramadan, which is a time of fasting and spiritual development. Every day of the month, Muslims who are physically capable are supposed to abstain from eating, drinking, and having sex from sunrise to sunset. A lot of devout Muslims also try to recite the entire Quran and offer extra prayers, particularly at night. Muslims generally believe that the Prophet Muhammad received his first revelation of the Quran during the last ten nights of Ramadan.

What is the connection between soul and body that the observance of Ramadan seeks to explain?

According to the Quran, fasting was advised for believers to increase their awareness of God. It is said that giving up items that most people take for granted, like water, might cause one to consider life's meaning and become nearer to the one who created and maintains everything. Therefore, breaking the fast is effectively undermined by wrongdoing. Additionally, a lot of Muslims say that experiencing hardship via fasting helps them become more empathetic.

Can Muslims break their fasts in some situations? If so, do they compensate for days lost?

Everyone who is physically unable to fast (because of an illness or advanced age, for example) is released from this responsibility; this also applies to anyone who is traveling. It is expected of those who can do so to make up the lost days at a later date. It is possible to make up for lost time in the month of

Shawwal, which comes right after Ramadan. If they have the means, those who are unable to fast at all are supposed to provide food to the less fortunate as an alternative.

What does it mean to fast for 29 or 30 days?

Muslims who observe prolonged fasts want to develop particular attitudes and ideals that they hope to be able to maintain for the entire year. Many compare Ramadan to a spiritual boot camp.

In addition to experiencing hunger and thirst, believers frequently struggle with exhaustion as a result of early-morning meals and late-night prayers. This is particularly valid on the last ten evenings of the month. Not only was this the time when the Quran was said to have been revealed for the first time, but it was also when divine rewards were supposed to be increased. During this time, many Muslims will offer extra prayers.

Health Benefits and Challenges of Fasting

In addition to fulfilling Muslims' religious duties during the holy month of Ramadan, fasting offers numerous health advantages. Fasting has gained popularity as the go-to strategy for maintaining youthful appearance, physical fitness, and overall health. Benefits include better blood cell regeneration, better weight management, and enhanced heart health.

But if you're not aware of just a few of the many advantages of fasting, here are some of them:

detoxifying

For a few days, giving up all solid food and living only on liquids is an excellent method to detoxify and cleanse the body. This improves organ function, supports a clean digestive system, increases blood flow, and gets rid of any dangerous pollutants.

suppressive of appetite

Have you ever had the impression that you are unable to recognize when you are satisfied? or just eating because you're bored? Fasting is one way to address those issues. Your body gradually adjusts to not being hungry all the time if you plan your day around everything but eating. Many Muslims who observe the mandatory fasts during the holy month of Ramadan may discover that they are unable to satisfy their appetites on the fasting day. They therefore break their fast. This is because, over time, your stomach decreases in proportion to the amount of food you put in it, making you feel full after just a short meal.

Over time, a few days of intermittent fasting can significantly reduce appetite as our bodies adjust to our eating schedule. You feel fuller after a smaller meal than normal since the human body can't comfortably digest a substantial quantity after breaking the fast. Additionally, your body produces more thyroid hormone as a result of this process, which raises your metabolism.

The metabolic process

Fasting reduces obesity, which is one of the most noticeable effects of the practice. The liver's enzymes break down lipids and cholesterol to produce bile acid, which then turns into heat and accelerates metabolism. Naturally, reducing one's appetite also lowers one's body's levels of the hunger hormone. After a fast, you might discover that your portion sizes have drastically decreased.

Loss of Weight

Fasting is the practice of abstaining from food, liquids, or perhaps both at the same time. The human body converts to fat during the hunger process to use and burn any stored energy first.

When followed properly, fasting can be a very effective way to lose weight, especially when it comes to the body's fatty tissues being shed, which improves overall physical structure. A regular resistance exercise program that includes intermittent fasting will encourage higher fat reduction with faster results.

Immune System

Fasting helps the body heal by directing its energy toward the immune system and metabolism rather than digestion, which in turn helps the body build more muscle.

White blood cells make up the majority of the immune system, and fasting helps your body recycle any old white blood cells, which builds a stronger, healthier immune system. When your body starts consuming food again, your body produces new red, white, and platelet-containing stem cells.

Blood Pressure

Blood pressure is lowered when the body consumes less salt and loses salt through urine.

Training

Human growth hormone, or HGH, is a hormone that the body naturally produces. It is well known for its ability to increase muscular mass, which helps the body burn fat. Even while it only stays in your bloodstream for a short while, it can significantly improve lean muscle strength, which could be very helpful for training.

Before major games, many athletes make use of the fasting approach since it's essential for burning fat and maximizing muscular building.

Enhanced Heart Function

A healthier heart can result from fasting, which also lowers cholesterol and increases blood vessel growth and muscle performance.

Mental Well-Being

Additionally, fasting has a profoundly positive impact on mental stress reduction and mental balance. Fasting has also been shown to improve mental clarity, strength, and focus. This is mostly because fewer calories, sugar, and salt are consumed during the fast.

Blood Sugar

Because glucose levels are stabilized during the fasting phase, type 2 diabetes may be avoided as a consequence.

Radiant Complexion /Anti-ageing

Fasting has been suggested to have the ability to extend one's youth and physical fitness as well as to slow down the aging process. The human body breaks down superfluous cells during a fast to produce repaired tissues and cells. You can manufacture collagen as a result, which will result in skin that is healthier and more radiant.

Healthier Brain and Cognitive Function

Blood in the human body contains more endorphins throughout the fasting process, which promotes mental clarity and a sense of well-being. Overall, fasting affects the brain which is comparable to that of exercise.

All capable Muslims are required to fast during the month of Ramadan since it is one of the five major tenets of Islam.

But, it's crucial to keep in mind to properly organize your fasting structure if you want to include any other kinds of fasting at any other time of the year. To fully benefit from fasting, be realistic about your goals and make sure you are in a state of mind and body that is conducive to fasting. Always make sure you get enough sleep and maintain a low level of stress.

Recall that on the day of Eid-ul-Fitr, one of the two major Islamic holidays that comes after the holy month of Ramadan, it is prohibited to fast.

You may find our Ramadan calendar here, along with further details about when to fast throughout this auspicious month.

Intermittent fasting cautions and concerns

Intermittent fasting has potential, but not everyone should do it. Since a large portion of the research has been conducted on animals, it is unclear if humans will experience the same advantages. Furthermore, Hyer notes that the majority of early research focused on the more radical 5:2 diet. The benefits of limiting meals to eight or twelve hours per day are still being investigated by researchers.

Furthermore, some populations or individuals with specific medical conditions may find fasting to be inappropriate. Hyer advises against fasting (or consulting a physician beforehand) if you:
• Are above 65 years old
• Are still developing; that is, children, teenagers, and young adults
• Be suffering from diabetes
• Suffer from liver, renal, or heart disease
• Have a history of disordered eating or an eating problem
• Are nursing or pregnant?
• Have a low pulse rate
• Use drugs that alter your blood sugar, blood pressure, diuretics, blood thinners, or other conditions.

Tips for enhancing your well-being throughout Ramadan:

• **Enjoy a nutritious iftar** In addition to the inherent advantages of Ramadan, you must adopt healthy lifestyle choices. Your body receives an immediate energy and hydration boost when you break your fast with three dates and water before your main meal. Since it helps you stay hydrated, light soup is a great option to start your major Iftar meal. Limit the quantity of rich, creamy, and fried foods, as well as salty and sweet foods. Think about choosing leaner meats and fish, wholegrain or brown rice, pasta, and don't forget to consume your veggies! To prevent deficiencies, always give priority to vitamins like C and D. To improve digestion and avoid gaining weight, eat slowly and pay attention to your portion sizes.

• **Make Suhoor a nutritious meal** Suhoor ought to be the most significant meal of the day, much as breakfast. Nutrient-dense foods like oatmeal, cheese, labneh, fruits, and veggies can help you maintain a balanced Suhoor. Oats, quinoa, wholegrain and multigrain bread, hummus, and yogurt are among the foods with reduced glycemic index (low GI) that are smart choices since they release energy gradually throughout the day. Keep in mind that during the fasting hours, you should drink plenty of water, milk, laban, and fresh juices to stay hydrated instead of tea and coffee.

• **Drink plenty of water.** Dehydration is normal and might cause minor headaches and blurred vision. However, by consuming a lot of liquids during the Iftar and Suhoor hours, you can assist yourself stay hydrated. Drink lots of water or a light tea without sugar or milk; you can also add slices of lemon or fresh mint to help with digestion and detoxification. Try reducing your intake of coffee and fizzy drinks if you consume them frequently, as they are diuretics that cause the body to become dehydrated.

• **Engage in Moderate Exercise Dehydration** and fasting might naturally make you feel drowsy, which will make your Ramadan days inactive. On the other hand, you should aim to exercise in moderation along with maintaining an adequate fluid intake. Staying active can help you feel less exhausted, provide your body the energy it needs to continue, and, if necessary, help you lose weight. Exercise during the fasting period, however, can be hazardous and dehydrating. To get the most out of your workouts, it's better to work out right before Suhoor or a few hours after Iftar.

• **Adopt good habits (and break the bad ones):** Ramadan is an excellent time for you to give up bad habits like smoking or sugar. You can continue to abstain from your addictions both during and after the fasting hours if you exercise a little self-control. Additionally, Ramadan is a fantastic time to establish and uphold healthy habits like increasing your intake of vegetables, water, and exercise.

Common challenges faced during Ramadan fasting

There are difficulties associated with fasting during Ramadan, but it's critical to address them with optimism and dedication to spiritual development.

Individuals can improve their Ramadan experience by effectively navigating the barriers of fasting by taking into account physical, social, and psychological elements.

Muslims throughout the world observe intensified dedication, self-discipline, and introspection as the holy month of Ramadan draws near. Important customs during Ramadan include abstaining from food and liquids and fasting from sunrise until sunset. Fasting has its own set of difficulties even if it is revered and regarded as beneficial. This blog post will look at typical problems that arise during the fasting month of Ramadan and offer solutions.

Adult Muslims who follow the fast are not allowed to eat or drink anything from sunrise to sundown during Ramadan. To sustain energy levels, it's critical to drink plenty of water throughout non-fasting hours, eat wholesome meals during Suhoor (the predawn meal), and engage in mild exercise. Fasting might be more comfortable if you get enough sleep and take care of yourself.

In areas where Ramadan falls during months with more daylight hours, fasting during the holy month might be extended. This can be especially difficult for people who live in areas with longer daylight hours.

The lengthy fasting time can be made more manageable by carefully organizing meals, beginning the fast with hydrating fruits and water, and taking it slow during Iftar (the evening meal). Furthermore, it could be beneficial to modify daily plans to save energy during the hours of fasting.

Balancing Spiritual and Social Commitments

It can be difficult to juggle commitments to your family, job, and social life during Ramadan. Professional and social obligations may clash with the desire to fully immerse oneself in spiritual activity.

Finding a balance between social and spiritual obligations, setting priorities for your work, and being honest with friends and coworkers about the meaning of the holiday are all crucial for managing expectations and lowering stress during Ramadan. There are other advantages to spending weekends and vacation days in spiritual pursuits.

For those who are fasting, social events—especially ones that center around food—can be challenging. One's ability to resist the urge to eat during non-fasting hours may be tested.

Navigating social pressures can be facilitated by having discussions with friends and family about the importance of promoting the fasting person, choosing healthier foods for Iftar, and accepting moderation. Refusing temptations can also be aided by cultivating mental discipline via exercises like prayer and meditation.

Concentration and productivity may be impacted by the dietary and sleep modifications made during Ramadan, particularly in a work or educational setting.

It is beneficial to schedule duties at times of increased alertness, take brief pauses for prayer or rest, and keep lines of communication open with managers or educators about any potential difficulties to reduce the impact on work or academic performance. Furthermore, highlighting Ramadan's spiritual advantages might serve as inspiration.

THE Ten Youthful Ramadan Challenges And Their Fixes

Ten obstacles that young people may encounter during Ramadan are listed below. The first step to conquering such obstacles, no matter how overwhelming they may seem to you, is to have unwavering trust in your Lord the Omnipotent and declare, "Yes, by God's Power, I can overcome them all!"After that, you'll begin your Ramadan journey with the motivation and optimism you need to conquer every obstacle, resist any temptation, and accomplish any objective during the month of Ramadan.

1. laziness and a lack of drive, patience, and endurance to observe the Ramadan rituals, particularly the standing for the entire tarawih and the complete fasting of the day

Solution: Give your Lord Almighty a lot of du'a so that He can give you all the strength and endurance you require. And discover the innumerable advantages and unique rewards of Ramadan to maintain focus and obtain the necessary inspiration.

2. Hunger, thirst, and tiredness due to a long day at school with a lot of classes and sometimes physical activities

Solution: Eat suhur at the optimal time, which is just before the Fajr prayer. You should also have a nutritious meal and enough water to stay well-hydrated while fasting. Additionally, refrain from engaging in excessive physical activity, and keep in mind that you are free to request a religious exemption from your school during Ramadan. Recall that experiencing hunger and thirst is a natural aspect of fasting, therefore these feelings are beneficial rather than detrimental.

3. Lack of sleep due to late long tarawih, very early suhur, and early start of the school day

One way to address this is to create a timetable that prioritizes things like education, prayer, the Quran, dhikr, tarawih, suhur, and so on. Use your time wisely and avoid wasting it on pointless activities like using technology excessively.

4. Absence of concentration

Answer: Think of fasting as an increase in mental clarity and focus rather than a decrease due to reduced food intake and increased spirituality. Eating and drinking generally induce drowsiness and laziness.

5. temptations to do evil in the classroom, online, and elsewhere

The best course of action is to stay as far away from any situations or events—whether at school or outside—where there are temptations to sin. You should also try to limit your usage of devices and avoid pointless online browsing.

6. Observing people consume food and beverages in front of you, especially at school, and engaging in activities that you are supposed to abstain from throughout Ramadan

Solution: Express gratitude that you are being prompted to fast and offer prayers for others to be guided as well. Do not feel guilty or like you are missing out on food or drink. Ask the administration to allow you to go somewhere else, like the library, if it's lunchtime instead of the cafeteria; they can make this concession if you have a valid religious reason.

7. being confronted with inquiries such as: (1) "Why are you unable to consume even water?"(2) "What is the purpose of your self-torture?", (3) "Why put oneself through suffering while fasting?"

Solution: find out what the appropriate responses are, then politely and respectfully give them. The following are the answers: (1) I am unable to even drink water during a fast because, according to Islam, a person may only truly and completely practice self-control during a fast when they abstain from all food, beverages, and sexual activity to attain both physical and spiritual self-purification. (2) and (3) There is no pain or misery involved in fasting. Rather, it is a constructive, demanding, and fruitful endeavor that will atone for my sins, strengthen my faith, enhance my physical and mental well-being, increase my vitality, and bring me closer to my Lord and His love.

8. Tempted to follow advice like, "Just break your fast and don't worry, nobody is watching!"
The answer is always God, the All-Seeing, All-Watchful!

9. juggling the Ramadan timetable with the academic calendar

One possible solution is to create a timetable that balances the lowest amount of academics required with the minimum amount of Ramadan commitments. Then, ask God Almighty to bless you for adhering to this schedule and enabling you to accomplish a lot in a shorter amount of time. The good news is that God the Most Generous will still give you the highest and entire recompense even if you truly do your hardest but are unable to achieve a perfect balance!

10. It is necessary to inform non-Muslims about Islamic fasting during Ramadan.

Solution: You ought to see this obstacle as a gift and a wonderful chance to spread Islam. Just make sure you know everything there is to know about fasting and Ramadan.

Chapter Two

Nutrition and Hydration Strategies

A common error made by many is to alter their healthy diet for the rest of the year to fit their Ramadan schedule. However, the truth is that there are numerous advantages to eating a balanced diet throughout Ramadan. During Ramadan, making healthy meal choices can help with blood pressure, diabetes, high cholesterol, weight loss, and other conditions. While there are many tasty, high-calorie meals and treats available during Ramadan, it is advised to consume them in moderation to maintain good health and prevent issues. Rich, greasy, or fried foods might contribute to a lethargic and fatigued feeling. As a result, it's critical to follow a Ramadan meal plan that addresses your nutritional needs.

Eat foods high in proteins, carbs, vitamins, and minerals during Ramadan to satisfy your body's energy and nutritional needs. In addition, you must exercise caution to avoid consuming too much food at once during Suhoor. By doing this, the body is prevented from utilizing all of the energy it uses up at once, which may result in weight gain.

Along with your Ramadan diet, you should aim to consume three to four liters of water each day. You must drink 1.5 to 2.5 liters of water a day, even if 40% of it comes from food, fruit juices, bottled water, tea, and other drinks. This implies that from Iftaar to Suhoor, you should have two to three glasses of water per hour.

What Is a Healthy Ramadan Diet Requirement for Iftaar?

You can adhere to a healthy Ramadan meal plan by using the Iftaar suggestions provided below to ensure that your needs for adequate nourishment during Ramadan are met.

• To begin, have a glass of laban or water and some dates. This may prevent dyspepsia. After a brief interval, have your main meal. To prevent getting a cold, make sure you consume water slowly and at room temperature. Drinking cold water also narrows blood vessels, which contributes to heartburn.

• Healthy foods should be the major course of your Ramadan diet. It should comprise a healthy, well-balanced diet that includes a variety of food groups, as each has special advantages. Don't overindulge; instead, eat each item in moderation. Grain, legumes, meat, dairy, fruits, and vegetables are foods you should eat.

• It was advised that as part of your Ramadan diet, stay away from caffeinated liquids like tea and coffee.

• Vegetable soup is a great place to start because it provides your body with the necessary nutrients, vitamins, minerals, and dietary fiber. Additionally, soup promotes digestion, keeps you from becoming constipated, and makes you feel full.

• You can eat foods like chicken and legumes like kidney or black beans throughout Ramadan to ensure that your diet also contains enough protein. You can eat items like rice, bread, pasta, and potatoes to get carbs.

What Should You Include In Suhoor For A Healthy Ramadan Diet

Eating a nutritious meal for Suhoor during Ramadan will help stave off headaches and weariness in addition to slaking extreme thirst. Ideally, the foods you include in your Ramadan meal plans for Suhoor will help you feel fuller for longer.

• Nutritious meals including cereals and dairy (unsalted) should be included in a balanced suhoor meal.

• Along with foods high in protein, like eggs, your meal should also include fruits and vegetables to ensure you are getting enough fiber.

• Ideally, you should stay away from salty foods including pickles, salty meals, olives, salty cheeses, spices, and seasonings. Consuming an excessive amount of sugar throughout your suhoor diet is not advised either.

When it comes to a nutritious snack between Iftaar and Suhoor, you can't go wrong with some fruit, fruit yogurt, or unsalted nuts.

What Advantages Do Healthy Foods Offer During Ramadan?

Muslims are obligated by religion to fast throughout the holy month of Ramadan, but when coupled with a nutritious diet, fasting can have several positive health effects. **The following are some possible health advantages of maintaining a nutritious diet while fasting during Ramadan:**

•   **Enhanced Insulin Sensitivity:** Fasting throughout Ramadan can enhance insulin sensitivity, which helps minimize the risk of type 2 diabetes and enhance blood sugar regulation in general. Your body must use its reserves of fat and glycogen to power itself during a fast. Insulin resistance can be decreased and insulin sensitivity raised by this mechanism.

• **Weight Loss:** If a person maintains a healthy diet during the non-fasting hours of Ramadan, fasting during the month of Ramadan can aid in weight loss. You might be able to achieve a calorie deficit that results in weight loss by eating less and going longer between meals. To make sure you're obtaining the nutrients your body needs during the non-fasting hours, it's crucial to keep up a nutritious diet.

• **Better Heart Health:** By lowering blood pressure and cholesterol, fasting can help strengthen the heart. According to certain research, fasting can lower blood pressure, reduce inflammation, and improve lipid profiles, all of which can minimize the risk of heart disease.

• **Decreased Inflammation:** Asthma and arthritis symptoms may be lessened by fasting's ability to lower the body's inflammatory response. According to some research, fasting can lower the body's inflammatory indicators, which may be advantageous for people who suffer from chronic inflammatory diseases.

• **Better Brain Function:** Research indicates that fasting may lower the risk of neurodegenerative illnesses like Alzheimer's and enhance cognitive performance. Fasting may encourage the brain's new nerve cells to proliferate, which could enhance cognitive function and brain function.

It's critical to keep a nutritious diet during the non-fasting hours of Ramadan to optimize the health benefits of fasting. This entails staying away from high-fat and high-sugar foods and choosing whole foods instead, such as fruits, vegetables, whole grains, lean protein, and healthy fats. During the hours when you are not fasting, it's also critical to maintain proper hydration by drinking lots of water. To maintain energy levels throughout the evening, it's also critical to break the fast with a small supper that combines complex carbohydrates, protein, and healthy fats. Fasting during Ramadan can have several health benefits, as long as one follows a healthy diet and stays hydrated.

Physical Activity and Exercise

The Ideal Time To Exercise During Ramadan

The ideal time to work out during Ramadan varies from person to person and might be a personal choice. I would suggest planning your workout for right before one of your meals during Ramadan, such as right before iftar or right before suhoor, to make things easier for you.

My 10- to 20-minute workouts throughout Ramadan make it quite doable before Iftar, which is something I strongly advocate. You'll have time to shower and get ready for dinner this way. Be sure to prepare your iftar meal in advance if you decide to work out just before the meal.

Try working out after iftar if you have a busy schedule or work in an office full-time. Since iftar times can change, especially for people in the UK, schedule a couple of hours for your body to process food before doing a little workout. You can replenish your energy later on with a nutritious snack. If preparing for iftar and job take up a lot of your evenings, this strategy might be most effective for you.

An alternative would be to work out before Suhoor to nourish your body before the start of the fasting period. The greatest times to work out throughout Ramadan are during these periods; which hour you choose will depend on your lifestyle and schedule in general. Staying constant will be easy if you make the right decision.

How To Maintain A Workout Routine During Ramadan

The following simple actions will assist you in staying on course:

1. Select the Appropriate Workout Period:

Choosing the right time to exercise throughout Ramadan is essential. Although everyone has a different ideal time, choosing this is an important first step. Exercise at the appropriate time guarantees consistency; trying to work out at the incorrect time might be difficult and discouraging.

2. Choose Brief Exercises:

For people with tight schedules, short workouts are a game-changer, not just during Ramadan but even outside of it. To make it more doable and reduce the sense that it's a heavy chore, choose short sessions (10–20 minutes) despite the possibility of decreased energy levels throughout this month.

3. Pay Attention to Your Body:

Keep an eye on your energy levels and observe how your body reacts. If you're feeling tired, think about doing less strenuous things or delaying more strenuous exercise until after you're not fasting. Striking too hard could make you reluctant to work out throughout Ramadan, which could throw you off course.

4. Show Flexibility:

Accept that there can be more difficulties on some days than others. Be adaptable and modify your exercise regimen as necessary. Maintaining consistency requires flexibility, particularly during a month with specific responsibilities.

5. Set Realistic Goals:

Adapt your exercise objectives to the unique demands of Ramadan. Focus on sustaining consistency rather than setting lofty goals. This guarantees that you won't experience needless pressure while you continue on your fitness path.

Best Type Of Workouts To Do During Ramadan

It is best to stick with moderately intense workouts during Ramadan. Depending on when you schedule your workout, the kinds of workouts you usually perform outside of Ramadan may vary, but here's a quick summary of some of the greatest options to think about doing throughout this unique month:

Mode Of Exercise Throughout Ramadan

1. Cardiovascular Workouts:

• **Brisk walking:** This low-impact exercise raises heart rate without making you feel too exhausted.

• Riding a bike

2. Exercises Using Your Bodyweight:

• Push-Ups

• Lunges and Squats

• Boards

3. Extending:

• **Stretching Exercises: Ideal to perform before Suhoor**

4. Exercise for Strength:

• **Light Resistance Training:** To preserve muscular mass, use light dumbbells or resistance bands.

• **Exercises for Bodyweight Strength**

5. Swimming:

• **If at all possible, swim:** For those who have access to a pool, swimming provides a low-impact, full-body workout.

6. After-Iftar strolls:

• Light Walking: You might want to take a stroll after Iftar. It's a low-impact method of improving digestion and getting some exercise.

7. Body-Mind Exercises:

• Pilates: Emphasised on body awareness, flexibility, and core strength.

Chapter Three

Sleep and Rest Patterns

Everybody fasts for a certain amount of the day and sleeps. Usually, these times for sleeping and fasting coincide. Your body goes into a special metabolic state while you fast and sleep. When you fast and sleep together, you give your body, mind, and digestive system the rest they need. Additionally, sleep and intermittent fasting are critical for preserving a balanced metabolic profile and a circadian rhythm that is in balance.

Based on a 24-hour diurnal light and dark cycle, humans have an intrinsic circadian rhythm that regulates everything from hormone levels to energy generation. Your body functions like a network of circadian clocks, and messing with these clocks' preferred "light = active" and "dark = rest" cycles can lead to sleep disorders, exhaustion, and even more dangerous health outcomes like cardiovascular disease. Another signal your body uses to keep these clocks in sync is intermittent fasting.

Strategies for maintaining healthy sleep patterns during Ramadan

Typical consequences of sleep deprivation and strategies to avoid them

Maintaining our general welfare, daily health, and capacity to perform well during the day all depend on getting adequate sleep. Our regular sleep schedules can be disturbed during the Holy Month by social events and activities, which frequently last late into the night. This may change the way we eat and sleep, which could result in insomnia. It can also interfere with our biological clocks and have a variety of negative effects on our overall health.

• **Mood fluctuations and headaches**

Our circadian rhythm, an internal 24-hour clock that regulates when we go to sleep and get up, is maintained by our body. Any variations in our sleep schedule can throw off this rhythm, which frequently leads to mood swings, irritability, and, in some cases, an increased risk of headaches and migraines.

• **Effect on mental abilities**

Getting enough sleep facilitates clear thinking, information retention and memory, and decision-making. Lack of sleep slows down our reaction speeds, makes it harder to focus and pay attention fully, and can even affect our ability to be creative and solve problems.

• **Gaining weight**

Dr. Muneer Alobeidli, the Program Lead for Caregiver Wellbeing at Cleveland Clinic Abu Dhabi, states that sleep loss alters the hormones that regulate hunger and appetite. Lack of sleep not only causes hunger sensations but also impairs judgment when it comes to what you eat, which frequently results in giving in to desires for sugary, fatty junk food and increases the likelihood of weight gain.

Tips for better sleep during Ramadan

• **Attempt to obtain restful sleep.**

To acquire enough sleep, longer sleep blocks are preferable to several quick naps. After Iftar, try to obtain at least 4 hours of sleep at night before rising for Suhoor and Fajr. Then, go back to sleep for a few hours before rising for the next day.

• **Attempt to control your sleeping schedule.**

To ensure that you sleep and wake up at around the same time every day during Ramadan, consider scheduling a modified sleep schedule. This will facilitate the body's natural rhythm for a deeper, more peaceful slumber.

• **Take a little power snooze**

• If your energy and concentration are waning, taking a 20-minute power nap in the afternoon can help. If you find yourself oversleeping and feeling even more sleepy than before your nap, set an alarm.

• **Keep an eye on what you consume.**

At Iftar, stay away from heavy, fatty, or sugary foods as these can cause your body to work extra to digest your meal, disrupting your sleep. Avoiding coffee for many hours before bedtime can also help promote a restful sleep. Extremely spicy foods can also be detrimental to a good night's sleep because they can create heartburn and gas.

• **A comfortable sleeping space**

A calm, dark place is the best for getting to sleep and staying asleep. Refrain from using electronics like your laptop, phone, and TV right before bed because research indicates that the blue light they emit can disrupt your sleep.

Importance of rest for overall well-being

Stress has emerged as one of the major health issues facing people in the modern world. Research has shown that excessive stress can cause cardiac problems, cardiovascular illness, high blood pressure, chronic pain, insomnia, and even play a part in dementia and seizures. More people than ever before are living in a condition of perpetual stress.

People's health is only becoming worse since they are under more stress than ever before. In today's high-stress environment, eating well, staying hydrated, and exercising are all crucial to sustaining good health—but so is getting enough sleep. In actuality, nothing mitigates the damaging effects of stress quite like relaxation and slumber.

The majority of people are aware that increasing their level of relaxation and sleep is beneficial to their overall well-being. What most people don't realize, though, is that there are a ton of various side benefits of relaxation that can truly enhance your general health and well-being. These are but a handful.

Heals Your Body

The human body is designed to function best in short bursts of activity. For this reason, even a brief pause might provide you with the energy boost you need to get through the day. Breaks are short stops from work, physical activity, or stressful situations. They enrich relationships, advance mental health, foster creativity, raise productivity, and enhance well-being by lowering stress and elevating mood.

Your unique needs will determine how much sleep you need. You might need to take more frequent breaks if you have trouble sleeping, are upset, or are stressed out.

Getting enough sleep facilitates your body's natural healing process and helps it achieve equilibrium. This is the time for your body to heal and rebuild.

Reduces Stress

Stress is a natural part of existence. While it could stimulate some, it feels more like a burden to others. The majority of definitions of stress refer to an external or internal challenge, disruption, or stimulation, as well as the physiological reaction or perception of a challenge. Prolonged stress weakens your immune system and raises your chance of illness.

Your body goes into fight-or-flight mode during stress, or physiological arousal, sharpening your senses in anticipation of danger. During this state, you might feel your heart rate and blood pressure rise, your digestion slow down, your hormone levels rise (like cortisol), and you might have additional reactions.

In prehistoric times, the body's primary survival mechanism was the fight-or-flight response. It made it possible for our forefathers to swiftly defend themselves against unimaginable situations. But in today's environment, this reaction can occur frequently and in a variety of circumstances.

The parasympathetic nervous system, which is active during rest, is the opposite of the sympathetic nervous system, which is responsible for the fight-or-flight response.

Boosts Creativity

You are inherently more creative when you take time to unwind and rejuvenate. Taking time off allows you to refuel. The calm times encourage introspection and help you overcome obstacles in your creative process.

Synchronous patterns of spontaneous brain activation during rest are measured by functional connectivity of brain data. You consequently encounter an expanding number of solutions to open-ended issues, including coming up with novel uses for objects.

Improves Productivity

Your brain is less functional when it is tired, just like other muscles. Resting sharpens your intellect, which is one reason Mondays are often packed with important activities or meetings. You're always more productive following a period of rest.

You will be able to work more productively when you return to your work after taking a break. If you want to increase productivity and have a stronger sense of success, set aside one day per week to unplug.

Enhances Decision Making

"Sleep on it" is a fitting phrase because getting enough sleep enhances your decision-making skills. Working continuously without breaks can impair your emotional capacity and decrease your ability to concentrate.

Daily and weekly scheduled breaks help you to refocus your thinking and ultimately help you make better judgments.

Sleep is important only when it is deliberately taken. These are some strategies that you can incorporate into your everyday routine.

Restful Techniques

Plot downtime in your calendar the same way you would a meeting or appointment, especially when life gets hectic and your to-do list gets long. Establishing easy daily habits that signal when to take a break can make unwinding much easier.

1. Be grateful for what you have

Refocus your gratitude on the small things instead of the "big" things, as most people like to do. Studies indicate that thinking positively and having gratitude in your mind can improve your mood and increase your level of life satisfaction.

2. Take Deep Breaths

Make it a point to inhale deeply five times a day. At various times during the day—for example, while your tea or coffee is brewing in the morning or while you're waiting for your computer to boot up—give yourself cues.

3. Cultivate Healthy Habits

Exercise elevates mood, balances hormones and neurotransmitters, and lessens the negative effects of stress. Try meditative exercises like yoga or stretching for the most zen.

Practice relaxation mindfully; it's a vital part of life and ought to be prioritized just like other to-dos and professional goals. Periodically shutting your body "off" can make a big difference in your mental, emotional, and physical well-being.

4. Practice Sleep Hygiene

Sleep is essential for both mental and physical well-being. A lot of the time, healthy behaviors lead to better sleep. By improving your daily routines, pre-bedtime routine, and sleep schedule, you may practice sleep hygiene and create automatic, high-quality sleep.

Establish a regular sleep routine that includes set wake-up times. Then, gradually change the sleep pattern as needed.

Have a set evening routine that you stick to. Engage in a pre-bedtime ritual that could involve spiritual uplift, such as meditation. Before going to bed, unplug any electronics and turn down the lights to facilitate your body's natural generation of melatonin.

Managing Stress and Mental Health

Ramadan's beneficial impact on mental health
One of the five pillars of Islam is fasting, which calls on Muslims to refrain from eating and drinking from sundown till sunrise.

It is always a good idea to see your doctor to find out if you should fast before doing so. If you are unable to fast, you can make a payment known as fidyah, which is the equivalent of two meals a day to a hungry and impoverished person.

How giving to charity and fasting improve mental health
Fasting is more than just giving up food. Along with avoiding offensive language like ignorance or indecency, you also refrain from engaging in destructive behaviors like fighting or arguing. This way, we may concentrate on cultivating positive behaviors and doing more good things.

To discover ways to bring our community together, there is a strong emphasis on charity and thinking of those in need throughout Ramadan. We begin to consider ways to give back and strengthen our relationships with our family and community during this month.

Such altruistic deeds have been demonstrated to increase endorphins, the neurotransmitter that makes us feel happy. Being philanthropic frequently coincides with an active, sociable lifestyle that can boost our self-esteem as we engage in worthwhile pursuits and help us fight feelings of isolation and loneliness.

Giving to charity causes us to feel good, which also helps us feel less stressed and distanced from unpleasant emotions like rage.

Ramadan offers us a chance to reset

We have the chance to address any unhealthy behaviors during the Holy Month. During Ramadan, you should take some time to consider and assess any bad habits you may have that you can change, such as smoking, drinking, using drugs, or using the internet excessively.

We can gain the spiritual capacity to examine our routines and actions during Ramadan. Furthermore, mastering the ability to abstain from harmful behaviors for the full day can help reset and strengthen one's resistance to triggers while simultaneously addressing desires and impulses.

How To Look After Your Mental Health During Ramadan

Ramadan is a crucial time for introspection and invigorating practices such as fasting, meditation, and prayer. But we also frequently notice adjustments to our daily schedules throughout this month, primarily as a result of changes in our eating and sleeping habits. Naturally, these changes may have an impact on our general mental and emotional health.

In these times, more than ever, we as individuals should put our mental health first by purging our minds of harmful substances and ideas and recharging them with thankfulness, kindness, love, and gratitude. I'll explain how.

Go easy on yourself. During Ramadan, self-compassion practice is crucial to enhancing our general well-being. We frequently disregard our bodies' requirements during the Holy Month due to the additional obligations it brings, which leaves us feeling stressed and overwhelmed. We all need to learn to be kind to ourselves and take breaks when we can. While it's true that we can all become overly consumed with obligations that consume a significant amount of our time and energy, it's important to never forget that we are only human and may occasionally need a quick break. It's critical that we all actively and deliberately cultivate the self-compassionate habit.

Challenge negative thoughts. Negative self-talk is a common human experience. However unfavorable ideas can damage our emotional health, undermine our self-worth, cause us to blame ourselves, and exacerbate anxiety and depressive emotions, all of which can result in an overwhelming emotional state. Take a step back, relax, and ask yourself whether these feelings are grounded in reality, whether there is proof to support them, and whether there are any other possible explanations or answers. This will help you overcome such situations. After you've responded to those inquiries, you'll experience a sudden, peaceful state of mind.

Avoid Burnout. It might get hectic during Ramadan. It's understandable that juggling your commitments to family and friends, keeping up with religious requirements, and attending innumerable iftar and suhoor events can become stressful and result in stress, anxiety, and exhaustion. What's the key to handling this? equilibrium. Striking a balance between our personal, social, and professional requirements is something that every one of us has to work on. It's okay to prioritize some time for yourself and occasionally cut back on your social obligations. Although Ramadan is a time to spend with loved ones, going to too many social events can be draining, and it's acceptable to acknowledge that.

Another option to consider is a reduction in working hours. Burnout can result from having the same amount of work but being behind schedule if it is not appropriately distributed. Even while work is undoubtedly your top priority, it's crucial to talk with your boss and coworkers to delegate tasks and make reasonable expectations to prevent any potential mental strain.

Get moving: The importance of exercise for our mental health cannot be overstated. Research indicates that physical activity causes fluctuations in the brain's chemical composition, including serotonin, stress hormones, and endorphins. These changes help to alleviate stress and anxiety while also enhancing mood. Make time in your day to engage in physical activity. Engaging in physical activities such as walking, jogging, yoga, or meditation can significantly improve your mental well-being.

Seek assistance: The majority of people, if not all of us, have gone through periods of emotional turmoil in our lives. This could occur as a result of significant life events or adjustments, difficulties encountered in our immediate surroundings, or ordinary annoyances and encounters. We attempt to manage these difficulties on our own by employing various coping mechanisms and getting support aids in the analysis, comprehension, and modification of coping mechanisms, if not the development of new ones. Speaking to someone else about your concerns or anything else that's been bothering you can be freeing and therapeutic. Although discussing your issues with close friends and family members can be quite beneficial, there are instances when those in your vicinity are unable to offer the necessary support. Never be afraid to consult professionals and licensed counselors, such as those on the Houna Initiative platform, for an outside viewpoint. Counselors and therapists with professional training can assist you in identifying the core of your issues, overcoming emotional obstacles, and implementing life-improving changes.

Practice Giving Back. In addition to fasting, Ramadan is a time for peace, prayer, and—above all—giving back to the community as a symbol of our gratitude and charity during this holy month. Giving helps us feel less stressed, depressed, and anxious. It also keeps our minds active, boosts our self-esteem, and gives us a sense of purpose, according to studies. Giving back to your community can take many forms: it can be as easy as smiling at people, helping at charitable events, or making financial contributions.

Engage in spiritual practices. Incorporating spiritual practices into our everyday routine can help us discover inner peace. Ramadan is a time for spiritual meditation and growth. Furthermore, spiritual activities can help people feel more connected to one another and as a group. Attending religious events can give us a sense of support and belonging, which is crucial for our mental health and general well-being. It can also make us feel more a part of our community.

A balanced diet. As basic as it may seem, eating a balanced meal and staying hydrated is essential for keeping up excellent physical and mental health throughout Ramadan. Physical and mental exhaustion can result from malnutrition and dehydration. Staying hydrated during non-fasting hours requires consuming a lot of water. Water facilitates digestion, helps control body temperature, and supports healthy bodily functions. A varied range of foods from several dietary groups, such as fruits, vegetables, whole grains, lean protein, and healthy fats, should be a part of a balanced diet. A balanced diet can lower the risk of disease, improve mood, and improve cognitive performance in addition to promoting physical and mental well-being.

Ramadan is a time for introspection, spiritual development, and personal development. During this time, it's critical to put our mental health first, handle stress, and lead a healthy lifestyle. We as individuals can make better progress during the auspicious month of Ramadan if we have a comprehensive plan and the appropriate resources. But as we all know, energy comes from more than simply the food we eat—it also comes from taking care of our minds and emotions.

Identifying common stressors during Ramadan

Islamic Perspective on Stress Management
Stress may be essential to human life, but too much of it can be harmful to our well-being and efficiency. It is estimated that approximately 20 million Americans experience stress to the extent that they attribute their sickness or its symptoms to it. The annual cost of stress-related compensation was close to $200 million. $50 billion is lost annually due to illness and productivity loss brought on by stress. Nearly $15 billion is spent annually by several businesses and individuals on employee stress management.

Medical research has sufficiently demonstrated the connection between stress and the development of depression, coronary artery disease, peptic ulcer disease, and hypertension. Furthermore, several prevalent issues, such as tension headaches, sleeplessness, impotence in males, and frigidity in women, are linked to stress to the development of diabetes, immune system suppression, and cancer. Stress has an impact on many aspects of our daily lives, including our eating and eating habits, work performance, grades, and home and family harmony.

Warning Signs Of Stress

Anger, mood swings, difficulty sleeping, inability to focus, stomach discomfort, excessive sensitivity to criticism, weight gain or loss, the anxiety of failing, poor appetite or hunger, and an increased reliance on alcohol or tranquilizers for sleep are some of the first indicators of stress.

Conditions Which Cause Stress

Over fifty stressors have been recognized by psychiatrists. In actuality, stress arises from any change—good or bad. Several events can cause a great deal of stress, including changes in employment or work description, school, housing, finances, family member or close friend loss or gain, illness or injury, news of riots or violence, and national tragedy. Muslims may experience more stress when they live in a non-Muslim society. These could involve things like maintaining their identity, practicing Islam (e.g., in food choices or prayer timing), defending Islam in the face of unfriendly media, resolving disputes within the family between the spouse, parents, and children, and practicing and non-practicing factions.

Are Easily Stressed

While stress affects everyone, even children, some professions experience higher-than-average levels of it. These include individuals who deal with complaint departments, salespeople, stock brokers, secretaries, inner-city schoolteachers, air traffic controllers, medical interns, and police officers. It's fascinating to notice that attributes that employers view as indicators of efficiency, such as being ambitious, compulsive, high achievers, and productivity-focused, are also type A personality traits that are extremely harmful to our health. Thus, the trick is to combine these traits with a laid-back type B mentality to extend your life and lead a happy existence.

Handling Stress

While stress is something we are all subjected to, why are some of us able to handle it better than others? Is it our innate nature or the way we respond to the stressor? There is research that suggests some of us may have a genetic predisposition to depression, lack neurotransmitter levels, or chemicals that regulate mood, or simply not make enough adrenalin when needed.

A person's personality and view on life are significantly influenced by his or her religious beliefs. A believer lessens his stress by placing his reliance on God, which absolves him of accountability and gives him less control over his shortcomings.

The methods used today to deal with stress include biofeedback, sociability, exercise, meditation, sleep, and tranquilizers. We will talk about stress management in light of the Quran and the Sunnah in this amazing book.

Factors of Stress

The following things contribute to psychological stress.

• A fear that stems from our incapacity to identify, anticipate, and manage the unknown.

• The loss of important items and persons in our lives, as well as our incapacity to come to terms with or accept these losses.

• Our blind spot regarding the future. If we could look into the future, we might even become more anxious.

• Disagreements between the mind and reality, as well as our inability to accept it (the denial phase).

Our internal conflicts cause us to lack inner peace, which disrupts our behavior and hurts our health.

Quranic Reflection on Stress Factors

Let's look at how the Quran handles these kinds of circumstances. For us, our losses are a part of the trial:

"Be sure We will test you with something of fear and hunger, some loss in goods or lives, but give glad tidings to those who are steadfast, who say when afflicted with calamity: To God we belong and to Him is our return. They are those on whom (descend) blessings from God and mercy and they are the ones that receive guidance." (Quran 2:55).

All that we own is a divine gift. They do not belong to us. All things are the property of God and return to Him. So why should we be proud to receive them or lament their loss if we don't own them?

God alone is aware of our final fate. We are unable to see into the future. We do, however, have a limited capacity for free will. We can choose to do good or bad, to believe in God or not, but we have no control over unrelated future events, such as whether my wife will give birth to a son or daughter, what color his or her eyes will be, or whether I will be in an accident tomorrow. It is useless to worry about matters like these.

Reflection on faith in the Quran is characterized as a sickness, with conceit and an unwillingness to embrace reality as its root cause.

"In their heart there is a disease and God has increased their disease and grievous is their penalty because they lie to themselves". (Quran 2:10

A man therefore creates an internal conflict between his heart and reason when he lies to himself. The mind instructs glands to secrete chemicals like adrenalin to quell the conflict, resulting in elevated heart rate, sweat, and tremors—the fundamentals of lie detector tests.

Big crimes like rejecting God or "small" crimes like adultery or stealing could be the cause of this conflict.

Chapter Four

Medical Considerations and Fasting

We are approaching Ramadan. For the millions of Muslims worldwide, it is an extremely sacred and spiritual period.

Islam has five pillars, and Zulfiqar Ahmed, M.D., an anesthesiologist in Beaumont, can't recall a day when he didn't observe the Ramadan fast.

"A lot of us do slow down during Ramadan," he stated. This is sort of me time. Despite being surrounded by others, we are all attempting to have a personal, one-on-one relationship with God."

Muslims will fast, pray, and congregate with loved ones for 30 days. During a fast, no food, liquids, or medications are consumed. However, what about people who have health issues? Do they have to participate in the fast?

In response, we go to another tenet of Islam: appreciating the blessings that God has bestowed upon you, including your physical self.

Dr. Ahmed said, "If someone is unable to participate, they don't have to." "Don't fast if it aggravates your medical condition. Take your medication if not taking it will harm you. It is neither expected nor appropriate to inflict wounds, agony, or injuries on oneself."

Fasting may help you manage your diabetes if you are following a diet. But if you need food and insulin to maintain acceptable blood sugar levels, take action. Maintain your health.

This also holds if you have received a cancer diagnosis.

According to Dr. Ahmed, "cancer treatment can bring significant stress on the body." "You should eat and stay in optimal shape rather than not eat and make your condition worse."

Dr. Ahmed went on to say that due to medicine, tests, and the severity of their condition, patients in the hospital definitely wouldn't be able to fast.

"Maybe if you're in the hospital for antibiotics only, you might be able to fast, but you probably shouldn't fast in the hospital," stated the doctor.

Additionally, remember to look after yourself if you're working hard outside on a sunny day. Accept the advice that your body is giving you. According to Dr. Ahmed, you may always make up for breaking your fast before sundown later in the year without losing your blessing if you have a valid reason for doing so.

Consult your doctor if you have recently received a diagnosis and are unsure about the implications of fasting. If you have any concerns about adjusting the times you take your prescriptions, you should also speak with your pharmacist or doctor.

"Fasting generally has incredibly beneficial impacts on the health and the soul. Individuals who have always fasted but are now unable to do so frequently miss it and feel guilty about it, according to Dr. Ahmed. "But we all should recognize that the body is a gift of God and we have to treat it with care."

Special Populations and Fasting

Ramadan, a spiritual period of the year during which Muslims worldwide intensify their worship and awareness of God, began this March. This entails offering prayers at night, reading passages from sacred texts, and fasting from food and liquids from dawn to dusk every day for the whole month.

In many religions, fasting is a common spiritual practice. On some days, especially Yom Kippur, the Day of Atonement, Jews observe fasts. For Lent, many Christians will fast, particularly on Ash Wednesday and Good Friday. The month of Ramadan is when Muslims observe fasting the most conspicuously. Because the Islamic calendar is based on the lunar cycle, Ramadan falls on an approximate date that is 10 days earlier each year than the widely used Gregorian calendar. Since daylight saving time has extended the days this year, many Muslims in the US will be fasting for as long as 12 or 13 hours every day.

Exemptions from fasting

Given how frequently Ramadan brings families together, it makes sense that kids would be excited about the holiday. As a religious or cultural practice, fasting can have a variety of advantages, such as self-sacrifice, discipline, a sense of social belonging, and a strengthened sense of faith.

However, it should be noted that in Islam, women who are breastfeeding or in menstruation, old or unwell, prepubescent children, and travelers are all considered religiously free from the requirement to fast.

No food may have negative consequences for these people. Dehydration, headaches, lightheadedness, dizziness, and syncope (fainting) are more common in these populations. Research indicates that fasting may result in a decreased production of milk and disruption of milk synthesis in nursing mothers.

Due to their smaller stature, greater surface area, higher metabolic needs, and inability to properly communicate or help themselves to food or drink, children can be more vulnerable to issues that occur from fasting. Fluids and a steady supply of energy are necessary for a child's body to remain healthy, especially for brain development. Even after a few hours, a person who is deprived of calories will see a decrease in glucose, the brain's primary energy source. This decrease in energy can lead to a variety of behavioral changes, from mild outbursts (which have been dubbed "hangry") to more serious issues including exhaustion and weakness. Even brief fasts have been demonstrated to impair cognitive function in children.

WHOM DOES SAWM EXEMPT?

Every Muslim who is sane, an adult, capable and a resident is required to fast. The exclusions listed below are applicable:

• the insane

• kids who have not reached adolescence yet;

• the old and chronically sick, for whom fasting is unreasonable; these individuals must provide food for at least one impoverished person each day of Ramadan, for which they have missed fasting.

• breastfeeding mothers and pregnant ladies may defer the fast till later;

• Travelers and the sick can also postpone their fast.

In Surah Al-Baqara of the Qur'an, Allah says:

However, if someone is sick or traveling, the allotted time should be made up a few days later. Allah does not wish to cause you any hardships; He wants to provide for you in every way.

• Women who are menstruating or who are confined after giving birth. It is not permitted to fast during certain times and should be made up day by day afterward.

To fast or not too fast

Muslims fast to emphasize the need to be grateful and to keep in mind those who are less fortunate. All fit adult Muslims are required to fast during the month of Ramadan as one of the five pillars, or responsibilities, of Islam. Exemptions include children who have not reached puberty, the elderly, people who are incapable of fasting due to medical or mental health issues, pregnant women, nursing mothers, and travelers.

Having said that, parents should carefully examine who should fast and for how long a child. Considering their child's health, activity level, appetite tolerance, and eating habits, parents should evaluate their child's capacity for fasting. Children should be included in the decision of whether or not to fast to foster a sense of belonging. For a youngster, shorter "practice fasts" or fasting from a particularly tasty food might be just as tough, while still teaching the needed patience and fortitude.

If children are fasting, parents should not expect a tiny child to fast a complete day from the outset. For smaller children, letting them fast for only a portion of the day helps him or her to feel included, but not excessively worried. Older children can increase the time of their fast in increments, which helps the child's body to acclimate.

When taking care of a child who is fasting, parents and other caretakers should bear the following in mind:

• For youngsters in particular, the morning meal, or "Suhoor," is a crucial component of the Ramadan fast, since families gather before dawn to partake in it. To feel fuller for longer, the meal should include high-fiber meals like whole wheat cereals, whole grains, legumes, fruit, and vegetables as well as high-protein foods like lean meats, nut butter, eggs, and dairy products.

• Children who fast should be urged to stay away from foods heavy in sugar because they will make them crave more and get less nutrition from them.

• To stay hydrated during non-fasting hours, children should also avoid high-intensity exercise, salty foods, and large amounts of fluid.

• Don't make them overeat during supper, sometimes called "iftar," to make up for the calorie deficit. Bloating, pain, and indigestion are the only effects of overindulging. Splitting meals may be a better option for kids to avoid food overload.

• To reduce stomach issues, fried, spicy, and carbonated beverages should also be avoided.

Eating a variety of foods from all dietary groups, such as fruits and vegetables, whole grains (cereals, brown pasta, breads), dairy products, meats, and healthy fats (olive oil, almonds, avocado), is crucial whether fasting or not.

Fasting guidelines for individuals with chronic illnesses

Many Muslims fast from sunrise to sunset as part of their religious commitment during the Islamic holy month of Ramadan. Healthy individuals can safely abstain from eating and/or drinking, even if it can be difficult at times.

However, if you have a persistent medical condition, fasting may make you more susceptible to consequences. "If you choose to fast and make any changes to your medication, your physician can advise you on these matters," says Henry Ford Health registered dietitian Allegra Picano, RDN.

When to Visit Your Physician Before Ramadan Fasting

For those suffering from a variety of chronic illnesses, such as:

• **Diabetes:** Individuals with poorly controlled Type 2 diabetes or insulin-dependent Type 1 diabetes may have hypoglycemia, or low blood sugar, during fasting periods. Additionally, they run the danger of developing ketoacidosis, a condition brought on by insufficient insulin in the body. Rather, the liver converts fats into acids (ketones), which have the potential to be fatal, to produce energy.

• **Chronic renal illness:** Fasting increases the risk of dehydration in persons with kidney disease, particularly in those with more severe conditions. It might potentially result in additional renal damage.

• **High blood pressure (hypertension):** To reduce extra water and sodium in their bodies, people with high blood pressure may take diuretics, or water pills. If they go for a prolonged period without drinking fluids, these people are more likely to become dehydrated.

• **Peptic ulcers:** Peptic ulcers are sores that form in the stomach and small intestine. If they are active, fasting might raise the risk of complications.

• **Cancer:** To preserve their energy and muscular mass, patients undergoing chemotherapy and other cancer therapies require more calories. It could be challenging to achieve these daily nutrient requirements while fasting.

Picano advises consulting your physician at least two weeks before the start of Ramadan to prevent difficulties from fasting. Your doctor can provide you with advice on:

• If you may safely observe a fast

• How to modify your medication's dosage or schedule while fasting

• How to monitor your health during a fast, such as by taking your blood pressure or sugar levels

Tips For Healthy Fasting During Ramadan

You can create a food plan ahead of time during Ramadan with the assistance of your doctor or dietician. Picano suggests using the following techniques during fasting:

• **Make nutrition a top priority.** Create a nutritious menu for the meal that is served before sunrise (Suhoor) and after sunset (Iftar). Select wholesome, satisfying meals that are high in fiber, such as whole grains, nuts, seeds, and beans. Consume fruits, vegetables, and lean proteins to acquire the vitamins, minerals, and energy you need for the whole day and night.

• **Steer clear of foods heavy in fat, sodium, and sugar.** This includes processed foods, refined carbs, and foods high in trans and saturated fats. Blood sugar spikes may result from certain foods. Consuming a lot of salty food can also raise blood pressure.

• **Remain hydrated:** Drink fluids, particularly water, during meals, in the evening, and in the early morning to avoid becoming dehydrated. Steer clear of caffeine, which can disrupt sleep, and sugary drinks, which can raise blood sugar levels.

• **Regulate meal quantities:** By controlling meals, you can prevent overindulging and gaining weight during Ramadan. To concentrate on savoring your meals and celebrations with loved ones, adopt mindful eating practices.

Indications That It's Time to Give Up Your Ramadan Fast

If you encounter any of the following illnesses or symptoms, Picano advises giving up fasting:

• **Low blood sugar:** If your blood sugar is less than 70 mg/dl, which raises the risk of hypoglycemia, break the fast. Keep an eye out for this condition's symptoms, which include confusion, dizziness, and a fast heartbeat.

• **Dehydration:** Keep a look out for signs like lightheadedness or dry lips, eyes, or mouth.

• **Difficulty generating urine:** Individuals with renal illness may experience difficulties generating urine when fasting, which may indicate dehydration and increase the risk of further issues.

• **Indications of an acute illness**: If you have trouble breathing, chest pain, disorientation, a high fever, or trauma, get medical attention right once.

"If you have any questions or concerns about your health during Ramadan, don't hesitate to contact your doctor," advises Picano.

Chapter Five

Social and Community Support

The Importance of Community During Ramadan

Without a doubt, Ramadan is a season when the community comes closer to Allah (SWT) and one another.

Since fasting is one of the five pillars of Islam, Muslims of all ages, backgrounds, and circumstances are united by the significance of fasting throughout the month of Ramadan.

During Ramadan, our communities participate in events that incorporate everyone in some way, whether it be large-scale Iftars, neighborhood street food vendors, or getting together for Taraweeh in nearby mosques!

In a similar vein, we collaborate during Ramadan to fulfill Zakat, another essential component of Islam. Giving to those in need has long been cherished by the Muslim community, dating back to the Prophet Muhammad (peace and blessings be upon him).

Since Ramadan offers the greatest chance to receive blessings from Allah (SWT), a lot of us decide to donate our Zakat or Sadaqah (charity) during this auspicious month.

Many Muslims get together to attempt and observe Laylatul Qadr, or the Night of Power, particularly during the final 10 nights of Ramadan. Laylatul Qadr is the best time for us to pray more and donate more to charity as a community because it is regarded as the holiest night of the year.

All community members get together to celebrate Eid-ul-Fitr, a joyful occasion for exchanging gifts, indulging in moderation, and spending time with our loved ones when Ramadan ends.

An auspicious period for introspection and more blessings, Ramadan is significant to every Muslim's life.

Ramadan is indeed a time when our spirituality, relationships with our family and community, and our ability to elevate our acts of devotion to Allah (SWT) all grow stronger and enable us to become the best versions of ourselves.

Utilizing the Power of Zakat is ideal throughout the holy month of Ramadan. For the benefit of Allah SWT, it is an opportunity for us to stop and think, replace bad habits with good ones, enhance our acts of worship and good deeds, and cultivate self-discipline.

Spiritual Reflection and Self-Care

Muslims fast, pray, and give to charity during the month of Ramadan to deepen their religion and enhance their well-being. It is also a time for communal introspection. Their general well-being and mental state may benefit from the habitual adjustments and heightened awareness that come with Ramadan.

Practices for self-reflection, gratitude, and mindfulness

The first day of Ramadan has arrived. Due to an extremely loud alarm, you wake up early for Suhoor, which requires you to have a few nibbles before the sun rises and your fast starts.

It's oatmeal for the night, some dates, and a glass of water today. This is perhaps the best Suhoor will get. You'll be lucky to get up early enough for just one date by the end of the month. You think, "I should work on developing a proper routine." You can connect to the impulse to reflect on yourself if you have celebrated Ramadan.

And it's time to do just that once more as April arrives this year. Ultimately, Islamic law mandates fasting as an act of thankfulness, based on the notion that depriving oneself of food and liquids will heighten consciousness of life's impermanent elements. In addition to allowing for introspection on one's blessings, voluntary hunger is intended to raise awareness of those who are less fortunate. Therefore, spiritual development is the cornerstone of Ramadan, even if it is typically linked with the physical discipline of fasting. Just as important as abstaining from food and water is refraining from gossip, swearing, and lying.

While most people believe that the hardest part of Ramadan is having to endure persistent hunger, the most difficult part is practicing mindfulness, which is either completely ignored or difficult to sustain. Thus, as feelings of thirst and hunger gradually subside over the month, seize the chance to redirect your attention toward establishing conscious objectives for even the smallest of acts; tiny changes help to reduce the process's frightening nature.

"One of the simplest things to do is incorporate meditation into your everyday practice. You can spend as little as five minutes on your couch. Put on your headphones, find a YouTube guided meditation video, and take some time to be alone yourself, says life coach Ms. Eshraf Kanfoud, who is located in Tunisia and is the first female mental trainer for an Arab professional football league.

She emphasizes that there isn't a single, universal approach to it. Islamic prayer schedules, which call for five daily prayers, can be excellent times for introspection and meditation. Writing in a notebook is a simple second. The most important lesson is that meditation can be any length of time you spend alone. It will make a difference if you dedicate two or twenty minutes each day to it.

The difficulty of achieving your goals will differ based on your location in the world. According to Kanfoud, "Working hours in Muslim countries usually decrease at the end of the month, which makes it easier to establish a regular schedule and allows you to try new things that you wouldn't normally have the time to do." "Being overseas makes it more difficult because your surroundings don't change, but the spirit of Ramadan can still inspire a desire for greater spirituality and mindfulness."

You are forced to focus on yourself when you meditate. It educates you to be aware of who you are. It can aid in your understanding of your sensations and ideas.

No matter where you live, Kanfoud maintains that cultivating mindfulness is an annual activity that is essential to mental well-being. However, Ramadan is a fantastic time to begin any time.

"It's crucial to keep in mind that meditation is the cornerstone of personal growth," continues Kanfoud. You are compelled to focus on yourself. It educates you to be aware of who you are. It can aid in your understanding of your thoughts and senses, which you can then organize, filter out the undesirable, and preserve the positive with practice.

Additionally, despite the common belief that exercise is impossible during a fast, it is not. Kanfoud recommends walking as a mild kind of exercise, which offers the added advantage of being a mindfulness exercise and an opportunity to reestablish a connection with the body. Kanfoud's counsel is endorsed by Mr. Ramu Mahrajan, a personal trainer at Dubai's 51 Gym. "Because you're probably going to be low on energy before breaking your fast, walking offers] an opportunity to re-establish a connection with yourself."

In the Arab world, it is customary for gyms to adjust their operating hours to allow for after-dark training. Mahrajan adds that there's no harm in doing out before breaking your fast as long as you don't overdo it, even if getting to the gym late at night is out of the question.

It's important to be gentle on your body because a month-long fast will eventually cause your energy levels to decline, according to Mahrajan. "Exercising vigorously while fasting will be too taxing."

Kanfoud agrees and restates that walking is the best option. "The brain, breath, and the steps you take synchronize with each other," she says. "You'll become more aware of that and the present moment as you walk more. You'll learn to live more in the moment and realize that you're not overthinking things as much.

Therefore, this Ramadan, even during your sleepy first Suhoor, it would be far better for you to spend a few minutes practicing mindfulness than overestimating the amount of work it would take to become a better version of yourself.

Nurturing the soul and fostering spiritual growth

Fasting's Spiritual Significance

Ramadan fasting has great spiritual advantages, purifying the soul of impurities and worldly wants. The Prophet Muhammad, peace be upon him, provided an example of why this month is sacred by saying:

"The gates of Hell are closed, the gates of Jannah are opened, and the devils are chained when Ramadan begins" (Al-Bukhari and Muslim).

The holy month of Ramadan is drawing near, and with it come many benefits and mercies. Forgiving sins is just one of the many benefits of fasting during Ramadan.

According to Abu Huraira, the Prophet Muhammad (PBUH) said:

"All previous sins will be forgiven for anyone who observes fasts during the month of Ramadan with sincere faith and the hope of attaining Allah's rewards" [Sahih al-Bukhari 38].

Fasting is associated with asking for forgiveness as well as being a deed that pleases Allah (SWT).

Abu Huraira recounts that the Prophet (PBUH) declared, "Allah said:

When he (the fast observer) abstains from food, drink, and sexual desire for My Sake, I will reward him for keeping the fast for Me. A person who is fasting will experience two pleasures: the first will come when they break their fast and the second will come when they see their Lord. Fasting is a screen (from Hell). Furthermore, according to Sahih al-Bukhari 7492, the scent of a fasting person's mouth is preferable to the smell of musk in Allah's eyes.

Tips for Balancing Work, Home, and Spiritual Obligations During Ramadan

It can be very difficult to be productive when working from home.

Throughout the day, a lot of items in the house might throw off the equilibrium you work so hard to keep. Now that the holy month of Ramadan has arrived, we have even more responsibility because of the particular duties we must perform.

"Ah, you who have faith! You are too fast, just as those who came before you were instructed to do so to achieve taqwaa [2:183].

Muslims throughout practice ibadah, which includes fasting and asking Allah for forgiveness and mercy, during this auspicious month. Being prepared is essential to keeping a regular work schedule and fulfilling your religious duties. These five suggestions will assist working professionals and their families in getting ready for an effective and prosperous Ramadan.

1. Establish precise objectives and action items. During the month of Ramadan, I established some very specific spiritual goals centered around my goals for my home-based business. Some are daily objectives, such as trying to arrive on time for every prayer, reading one chapter of the Qur'an a day, or taking part in the evening Taraweeh prayers. Limiting time-wasting habits, like watching television and using the computer, could be one of your weekly objectives. Longer-term monthly objectives could include throwing an iftar party at your house or improving a bad character characteristic. Your objectives should be clear, attainable, and quantifiable to track your development.

Mapping out your intended procedure from start to finish is one way to help you achieve a goal, like finishing the Qur'an. Calculate how long it will take you to read the complete Qur'an by the end of Ramadan by looking at your calendar. Decide to read one juz every day throughout Ramadan; there are 30 days and 30 ajiza. Writing down or scheduling this time on your calendar is crucial since it strengthens your resolve to accomplish your objective.

2. Make a plan beforehand.

An old proverb states, "Failing to plan is planning to fail." Consider all of your goals for the day and build a plan to achieve them. Create a short "to-do" list with all the things you want to get done this week and today. For instance, it might be helpful to plan your meals a week or two ahead of time, especially if you can double the recipe and freeze one of the meals for those days when everything seems to be too much to do. Suhoor and iftar meals can be planned for a week in advance, saving you the hassle of rushing to find something to eat for breakfast and dinner.

Planning and preparing family meals for a whole month may seem daunting, but it may save a lot of time, and money, and increase productivity. Make a list of the three full meals, two light, healthful snacks, and any beverages (lemonade, iced tea, etc.) you plan to serve each day for the next thirty days. Next, construct a grocery list with all the ingredients needed to prepare each of the meals and snacks you have listed. Get the ingredients and dedicate a weekend to cooking and preparing every dish. Carefully wrap the meals in large freezer bags or place them between freezer paper before putting them away in the freezer. The time, money, and energy you'll save by being able to swiftly pull a whole meal from your well-stocked freezer over the entire month of Ramadan will more than offset the sacrifice of one weekend.

3. Set priorities for your tasks.

Prioritize each item on your daily "to-do" list according to its significance. You may make sure you allot adequate time to complete urgent chores on time by organizing your projects according to importance. If necessary, you can set aside specific times during the day to finish particular activities. This is known as "time blocking" by a friend of mine, and it works incredibly well. It might be quite helpful to know that you have a set amount of time to focus on a task to reduce distractions and boost productivity.

Make a list of everything you have to get done that day to start. There is no set order in which the tasks must be listed. Next, give each task a letter reflecting its priority on a scale from "A" to "D." For instance, you may designate a "D" for folding clothes in the dryer because it may wait until the following day without having serious repercussions, and an "A" for waking your family for suhor and Fajr. Make a fresh list for the next day. You can choose to prioritize unfinished work more highly than you did the previous day.

4. Make sure your family is informed.

To avoid being bothered during business hours, establish clear boundaries with your family. You must successfully fulfill your professional commitments throughout Ramadan if your family's living expenditures are covered by your salary to fulfill your spiritual obligations and reach the objectives you have set for yourself.

It's a terrific family activity to get together and talk about how you're going to prepare for and observe Ramadan. Are there any particular things you want to work on getting better at during Ramadan, like managing your tongue and anger or refraining from backbiting and gossiping? This is an opportune moment to evaluate our character and contemplate any enhancements we may make. Talk about the many situations that could occur (such as dealing with slanderous coworkers) and assist in creating plans to steer clear of or manage them. Involving everyone boosts motivation and strengthens the family's as well as each person's objectives.

5. Just get started and don't delay!

It's quite simple to put off preparation when life is busy and Ramadan is quickly approaching, but before you know it, the first day of fasting will arrive! It's still not too late! Make the most of this auspicious month and prepare ahead of time for a fruitful and prosperous Ramadan so that you can benefit from the blessings Allah has granted in His boundless generosity.

• To make things seem less overwhelming, divide them into smaller, manageable chunks.

• Create a schedule with a deadline for every objective.

• Hang out with people who motivate you to get better and do things.

• Tell people about your objectives; they'll inquire about your progress and help you stay motivated.

• Commit to acting. If you don't take the required actions to get the intended outcome, your aims will be in vain.

Put an end to your procrastination and get ready right now!

What other strategies would you employ to balance the various facets of your life?

Chapter Six

Balancing Religious Observance and Health Goals

Islamic teachings are strongly rooted in the idea of balance (Mizan), which emphasizes moderation and harmony in all facets of life, including religious rituals and healthy lifestyle choices. Because of this, people must embrace Ramadan with a holistic perspective, understanding the connections between their spiritual, bodily, and emotional selves.

It takes a sophisticated grasp of both Islamic teachings and modern health standards to strike a balance between religious devotion and health objectives. A key component of Ramadan is fasting from sunrise to sunset, but Islam also places a strong emphasis on maintaining one's health and avoiding physical injury. Following the words of the Prophet Muhammad (peace be upon him), "There should be neither harming nor reciprocating harm." People are urged to take a proactive approach to their health and well-being and combine Islamic teachings with scientifically proven health practices to successfully strike this balance. This includes:

• **Seeking Knowledge:** Become knowledgeable about the dietary needs of fasting, the value of staying hydrated, and the advantages of a healthy diet and regular exercise during the month of Ramadan. People can choose their health-related habits with knowledge of the physiological consequences fasting has on the body.

• **Customizing Practices:** Understanding that every person has different health needs and that what is appropriate for one may not be for another. Customizing health practices based on an individual's age, health state, food preferences, and lifestyle variables is crucial.

• **Accepting Moderation:** Making an effort to observe moderation in all facets of Ramadan, such as sleeping, eating, and participating in religious events. While enjoying special meals and celebrations during Ramadan is normal, moderation is essential to prevent excess and uphold a balanced diet and way of life.

• **Making Self-Care a Priority:** Including self-care activities like mindfulness meditation, relaxing methods, and reaching out to others for support in everyday activities. During Ramadan, it's crucial to look after one's mental and emotional health in addition to one's physical health.

• **Consulting Experts:** To resolve any health problems or inquiries about fasting, seek advice from competent authorities such as medical specialists, religious scholars, and nutritionists. Expert consultation can help people strike a balance between their religious adherence and their health objectives by offering personalized guidance and assistance.

In the end, juggling health objectives with religious devotion throughout Ramadan is a voyage of personal development. People can foster their physical, mental, and spiritual well-being while experiencing the transformational power of Ramadan by embracing the fast with attention, mindfulness, and a dedication to holistic well-being. May this balance lead us to a happy and healthy Ramadan, as Allah tells us in the Quran, "And eat and drink, but be not excessive. Indeed, He likes not those who commit excess." (Quran 7:31).

You can create a wellness plan that is unique to you by comprehending the eight dimensions of well-being and how they affect general health. We will examine the various aspects of wellness, the environment's role in fostering wellness, and the tools at your disposal to help you on your path to a better lifestyle in this book.

Recognizing the Eight Wellness Dimensions

Being healthy is only one aspect of wellness; it affects all aspects of our lives. Physical, emotional, intellectual, social, professional, environmental, spiritual, and financial well-being are among the eight dimensions of well-being. To obtain optimal health, each dimension is interrelated and needs to be attended to.

To further appreciate each dimension's significance, let's examine it in more detail:

Physical Wellness

The physical aspect of wellness is about taking good care of your body by exercising, eating right, and getting enough sleep. Regular physical activity strengthens your cardiovascular system, increases muscular tone, and improves general flexibility in addition to helping you maintain a healthy weight. Furthermore, a balanced diet rich in different nutrients is necessary for the highest possible level of physical well-being. It helps avoid chronic diseases and gives your body the fuel it needs to perform correctly.

A good night's sleep is essential for maintaining physical health. Your body heals and regenerates itself when you sleep, supporting a strong immune system, emotional stability, and normal cognitive function.

Emotional Wellness

Emotional wellness depends on stress management and preserving mental health. Your general health can be greatly impacted by stress, which can also cause physical symptoms including headaches, tense muscles, and digestive problems. It's critical to develop good coping strategies for handling stress, such as relaxing exercises, taking up a hobby, or asking family, friends, or experts for assistance.

Developing a solid support network, strengthening resilience, and fostering happy emotions are all important aspects of maintaining healthy mental health. Emotional wellness can be enhanced by practicing gratitude, scheduling self-care activities, and partaking in joyful, fulfilling pursuits.

Recall that mental and physical health are intimately related. Regular physical activity can help lower stress and elevate mood, and maintaining mental health and stress management can have a favorable effect on physical well-being as well.

Intellectual Wellness

Taking part in mentally challenging and knowledge-expanding activities is a necessary component of intellectual wellness. It entails seeking lifelong learning, pushing your intellectual limits, and maintaining an open mind to fresh viewpoints. To improve intellectual wellness, one can read books, go to educational courses or seminars, and have thought-provoking discussions. You may maintain mental acuity and promote personal development by always learning new things and expanding your knowledge base. Being intellectually healthy enables you to think critically, adjust to changing circumstances, and make wise judgments.

Social Wellness

Since humans are social creatures, social well-being is critical to general health. It entails creating and preserving wholesome bonds, encouraging a feeling of community, and engaging in active participation in it. Strong social ties have been associated with better general health, lower stress levels, and higher levels of happiness.

Building deep connections, honing communication techniques, and participating in socially engaging activities are all crucial for improving social wellness. This can involve getting involved in groups that share your interests, volunteering, or joining clubs or organizations.

Occupational Wellness

Finding contentment and pleasure in your profession or chosen career path is referred to as occupational well-being. It entails feeling driven, experiencing a positive work-life balance, and possessing a sense of purpose. Your general well-being is positively impacted when you are content with your work.

It is crucial to choose a career that is in line with your beliefs, interests, and skill set to achieve occupational well-being. Keeping a good work-life balance is also essential to avoiding burnout and preserving general well-being. This may entail establishing limits, placing self-care first, and figuring out how to detach from work-related pressures when not at the office.

Environmental Wellness

The goal of environmental wellness is to establish and preserve a sustainable, healthy environment. It entails taking precautions to reduce damage and being conscious of how your actions affect the environment. This can involve cutting back on waste, encouraging eco-friendly activities, and conserving energy and water.

Furthermore, spending time outdoors and fostering a connection with nature might benefit your general well-being. Walking in a park, gardening, or participating in outdoor activities can all help lower stress, elevate mood, and improve mental and physical health.

Spiritual Wellness

Achieving spiritual wellness entails discovering connections, meaning, and purpose in life. It includes a larger sense of spirituality and personal values rather than just religious ideas. Participating in pursuits that are consistent with your principles, objectives, and life goals can enhance your spiritual well-being.

This can involve partaking in religious or spiritual rituals, practicing mindfulness or meditation, or taking part in activities that encourage introspection and personal development. Taking care of your spiritual health can provide you resilience, inner serenity, and a better understanding of both the outside world and yourself.

Financial Wellness

Having a positive relationship with money and feeling confident about your financial circumstances are considered aspects of financial wellness. It entails prudent financial management, goal-setting, and well-informed saving, spending, and investment choices.

A stable financial situation can ease anxiety and give you a sense of security, freeing you up to concentrate on other facets of your well-being. It's critical to form sound financial practices, such as creating a budget, setting aside money for emergencies, and getting expert guidance when necessary.

You can approach your general well-being in a more holistic and balanced way by being aware of and nourishing each aspect of wellness. Recall that maintaining your health is a lifelong process that calls for constant attention and work. Consider all aspects of your life and make deliberate decisions that will support your overall health.

Impact on Overall Health

Taking a comprehensive approach to wellness has a significant effect on our general well-being. Through the cultivation of each dimension, we can increase our longevity and raise our standard of living. Neglecting one component can have a cascading effect on other dimensions, resulting in imbalances and possible health problems.

Let's examine the components of well-being in more detail and see how they affect our general state of health.

Physical Wellness

Physical well-being includes taking good care of our bodies by exercising frequently, eating healthily, and getting enough sleep. Making physical well-being a priority boosts our vitality, fortifies our immune system, and lowers our chance of developing chronic illnesses. Strength training, flexibility training, and cardiovascular exercise are examples of physical activities that not only increase physical fitness but also elevate mood and facilitate better sleep.

Emotional Wellness

Effectively comprehending and controlling our emotions is the main goal of emotional well-being. It entails exercising self-care, cultivating wholesome connections, and creating healthy coping strategies. Setting emotional wellness as a top priority helps us develop inner peace, better manage stress, and feel better about ourselves. Positive thinking and emotional resilience can be developed by partaking in mindfulness exercises, counseling, and writing.

Cognitive Wellness

Maintaining mental acuity and engagement is essential to cognitive wellness. It includes mentally taxing pursuits like reading, picking up new skills, and solving puzzles. Prioritizing cognitive wellness improves our ability to concentrate, remember things, and solve problems. Learning a new language or playing strategy games are two examples of brain-stimulating activities that can help us retain cognitive function as we age.

Social Wellness

The goal of social wellness is to establish and preserve wholesome interpersonal interactions. It entails feeling like you belong, having empathy, and communicating well. Prioritizing social wellness enhances our general well-being, builds our network of support, and lessens feelings of loneliness. We can build deep relationships and improve our social well-being by taking part in activities like volunteering, joining clubs, and spending time with loved ones.

Spiritual Well-Being

Achieving spiritual wellness entails discovering life's meaning and purpose. It includes understanding our values, making connections with our inner selves, and doing things that are consistent with our convictions. Prioritizing spiritual well-being helps us develop resilience, thankfulness, and inner serenity. By meditating, practicing mindfulness, or spending time in nature, we can improve our general well-being and strengthen our spiritual connection.

Occupational Wellness

Finding contentment and fulfillment in our chosen job or place of employment is the main goal of occupational well-being. It entails keeping a good work-life balance, upgrading our abilities regularly, and matching our values and interests with our professional objectives. Prioritizing occupational wellness leads to a feeling of direction, drive, and personal development. We can improve our occupational wellness by partaking in activities like professional growth, seeking meaningful work, and establishing attainable goals.

Environmental Wellness

Living in peace with nature and taking care of our surroundings are essential components of environmental wellness. It includes maintaining a clean and safe environment, following sustainable practices, and being aware of our ecological footprint. Setting environmental well-being as a top priority benefits both the earth and ourselves personally. Recyclables, energy-savers, and outdoor enthusiasts can all contribute to environmental wellness by creating a sense of connection with the natural world.

Conclusion

As we approach the end of "Maintaining Health and Wellness During Ramadan," it is appropriate to take a moment to consider the path we have taken together. We have looked at the many facets of health and wellness throughout the holy month of Ramadan in this book, exploring the complex relationships between spiritual fulfillment, physical health, and religious adherence.

Ramadan provides Muslims with a great opportunity to strengthen their relationship with Allah, purify their spirits, and ask for forgiveness for past mistakes because of its emphasis on fasting, prayer, and self-discipline. But even amid all the spiritual zeal and dedication that accompany Ramadan, we must remember how important it is to take care of our bodies and minds to keep our health and well-being at their best during the fasting month.

We have looked at several topics related to maintaining good health throughout Ramadan, including exercise, sleep, stress reduction, medical concerns, and proper nutrition and hydration. People can reconcile their religious duties with their health objectives by combining Islamic teachings with scientifically proven health methods.

The core of Islamic teachings is the principle of moderation, or mizan, which is essential to maintaining this balance. By emulating the Prophet Muhammad (peace be upon him), who stressed moderation in all facets of life, we make an effort to achieve balance in our exercise routines, food choices, and spiritual pursuits. We can steer clear of excesses and develop a balanced, body- and soul-nourishing approach to the Ramadan fast by practicing moderation.

Furthermore, we have discussed the significance of practicing self-care and self-compassion throughout Ramadan, acknowledging that every person's journey is different and could involve difficulties. We may cultivate resilience and inner strength by making self-care activities a priority, such as mindfulness, relaxation, and reaching out for social support.

Let's use the knowledge and understanding we have obtained from this book in our Ramadan journey and beyond. I pray that we approach the fast with intention, mindfulness, and a dedication to our overall well-being, understanding that keeping healthy throughout Ramadan is not only a moral duty but also a profoundly transforming experience.

During Ramadan and throughout our lives, may we treat our bodies with compassion, respect, and thankfulness, as the Prophet Muhammad (peace be upon him) once said, "Take care of your body; it is the only place you have to live."

During this auspicious month, may Allah accept our fasting, prayers, and acts and give us strength, direction, and blessings as we travel the path to spiritual fulfillment, well-being, and health.

Happy Ramadan!

www.ingramcontent.com/pod-product-compliance
Lightning Source LLC
Chambersburg PA
CBHW070833260726
48660CB00005B/2042